Sergey Kuznetsov Architecture Drawings

Sergey Kuznetsov
Architecture Drawings

Edited by
Luca Molinari

Introductions by
Santiago Calatrava
Massimiliano Fuksas

SKIRA

Editor
Luca Molinari

Art Director
Marcello Francone

Design
Luigi Fiore

Editing
Emily Ligniti

Layout
Paola Ranzini

Translations
Sergio Knipe for *Scriptum*,
Rome

First published in Italy in 2014 by
Skira Editore S.p.A.
Palazzo Casati Stampa
via Torino 61
20123 Milano
Italy
www.skira.net

Printed and bound in Italy. First edition

ISBN: 978-88-572-2543-2

Distributed in USA, Canada, Central & South America by Rizzoli International Publications, Inc., 300 Park Avenue South, New York, NY 10010, USA.
Distributed elsewhere in the world by Thames and Hudson Ltd., 181A High Holborn, London WC1V 7QX, United Kingdom.

Contents

When I first had the opportunity to admire the drawings so beautifully illustrated in this volume published by Skira, I was gripped by emotion.

As I leafed through the text, I realized that my feelings were not simply due to the remarkable quality of the drawings, in which a dense yet graceful hand brings monuments and landscapes of unquestionable beauty to the reader's attention. The emotion I was experiencing had deeper roots, connected to the land the author has chosen as his field of research and testing ground. I am speaking of Italy and its remarkable art cities.

What emerges from these drawings by Sergey Kuznetsov is a desire to reclaim the original matrix of each work through the rendering of some of the most famous and interesting monuments in Italy, in such a way as to digest its components and get to the very roots of contemporary art.

To achieve this goal, Sergey Kuznetsov would appear to have drawn upon that "inner sight" described by Wassily Kandinsky, a sight which "penetrates the hard shell, the external form, into the interior of things and lets us perceive the inner pulsation of things with all our senses."

The collection of drawings featured here exudes the same feeling which inspired the great artists of the past to visit Italy, as illustrated by Stendhal in *Rome, Naples et Florence*, by Goethe in *Italienische Reise* or, indeed, by Joseph Brodsky when he speaks of the city of Venice in his poem *Lagoon*: "Mouldings and carvings, palaces and flights / of stairs. Look up: the lion smiles from heights / of a tower wrapped as in a coat / of wind".

This is the same city that Charles Dickens, after visiting St Mark's Square and its church, described to his friend John Forster as sumptuous and amazing, beyond all human imagination.

But celebrated modern writers are not alone in attesting to the charm of Italian architecture.

During the time he spent in Italy working on the set designs for the Russian ballet *Parade* – written by Cocteau and directed by Diaghilev – Picasso was strongly influenced by his visits to ancient monuments in Rome, Florence, Naples and Pompeii. From that moment, down to the mid-1920s, Picasso's encounter with ancient art shaped his oeuvre, as is shown by many works from this so-called "classical" period of his career, including the splendid *Flute de Pan*. Just like the Russian architect who is the author of the works illustrated in the present volume, during his short sojourn in Italy – where he met his great love, Olga Khokhlova – Picasso could not resist the impulse to capture the charm of the country's monuments through sketches and drawings.

I, myself, during my frequent trips to the capital of Italy, have behaved much like the Roman prince from Gogol's novel, who "each day would set out to discover new marvels and . . . stop when in a small piazza he chanced upon a picturesque fountain . . . or when a dark, dirty street ended with the playful architecture of Bernini, with a flying obelisk, with a church and the wall of a monastery which burst in the sun's brilliance on the dark azure sky, with cypresses black as coal. And the more he travelled the streets, the more palaces and architectural works by Bramante, Borromini, Sangallo, Della Porta, Vignola and Buonarroti emerged. Finally, he understood that only here, in Italy, does the presence of architecture become tangible."

No doubt, Italy is one of the most exemplary countries from the point of view of architecture, since it boasts a genuine historical repertoire for all the various ages in which architecture has played a fundamental role. This extends as far back as the Roman age, which has left grand works such as aqueducts, thermal baths, mausoleums and many other urban structures that are still to be found in Italian cities. Ultimately, Italy may be described as a country which has made its practice of architecture an exemplary one and which represents one of the world's leading schools for urban architecture.

On every visit I make to Italy, I will peer into the dense fabric of its art cities to discover a marble pediment set in a wall, a Doric column supporting a medieval architrave or a highly decorated baroque window. Pondering this prodigious mingling of styles, like the author of the sketches illustrated in this volume, I seek to capture the most concealed images and messages by drawing the founding elements of contemporaneity from the complex juxtaposition of different architectural languages. These repeated experiences, which I process through impromptu sketches and drawings, expand my own cultural background, while at the same time teach me to be humble in my own artistic pursuits.

Still, it is worth stressing that this constant drawing upon the roots of civilization on the part of modern and contemporary artists also entails a degree of profound reciprocity. If we take Russian artists, it is easy to see just how influential the music of Tchaikovsky, Stravinsky, Shostakovich and Prokofiev has been for twentieth-century European art. Likewise, the revolutionary ideas of Kandinsky and the movement he championed, Der blaue Reiter, paved the way for Bauhaus, the modern architecture movement which re-established a connection between art and real life. Or let us think here of how Vladimir Tatlin's Russian constructivism and Kazimir Malevich's early, visionary drawings inspired the young Antonio Sant'Elia, the author of the "Manifesto of Futurist Architecture".

One last point concerns the message that comes from the exhibition of these drawings. As Jean Dominique Ingres, Director of the French Academy in Italy, liked to say: "Le dessin c'est la probité dans l'art".

In a particularly delicate political moment such as the present one – in which the peoples of the West seem to have no memory of the damage and atrocities of past wars, and governments are fuelling a dangerous escalation by issuing reciprocal sanctions – the commitment displayed by Sergey Kuznetsov through the depiction of the artworks from a foreign country delivers a powerful message of integrity and peace. Such peace finds in the universal quality of art its lifeblood, and in the cultural exchange between different peoples its sole chance for survival.

Santiago Calatrava

"Drawing is nothing more than
an apparent expression and declaration of what one has in mind."
Giorgio Vasari

For some years now, the eternal debate over whether drawing is still an essential tool for understanding or the synthetic expression of concepts is being discussed again. At universities, especially American ones, which are the most culturally active, the translation of ideas by drawing has revived substantially. Too many years have passed since the Grand Tour in Italy gave artists the opportunity to photograph with cunning and graphic ability the remains of the past and history of the country. The extraordinary collection that Sergey Kuznetsov presents in this book is not only the proof we were waiting for about the ease of expression of some schools of thought, but also the graphic transposition of emotions quickly captured in an ideal trip that from Venice, passing to Santa Maria della Salute (pencil on paper, 2011) and San Zaccaria (ink on paper, 2009) then to Barcelona with the Mila house (brown ink and brush on paper, 2013) and Singapore (felt-tip pen on paper, 2013) and to the skyline of New York (Indian ink, brush or felt-tip pen on paper, 2014) seems to be linked with a thought. Urban spaces are a perfect representation of both the magic of the light changing during the entire span of the day and the clarity with which it shows the skilful strokes to outline the full and the empty. One might add that the urban voids, perfectly represented, are the very essence of the city. Only with time is one able to appreciate their importance. To start working from the idea of the void is a different experience. It means evaluating an item with a free value compared to the buildings that surround it. Giovanni Battista Piranesi said that drawing archaeological ruins had inspired his landscape nature, enabling the transition from a real insight to that which is more imaginary, fantastic and dreamlike. Today, travel notebooks are an irreplaceable tool to draw from and find motivation, just as for Le Corbusier, whose works refer to "forms" seen during his numerous trips and recorded in those famous carnets. Quick notes of the context taken from a train or from a ship or a more precise study of the buildings of the past until the recent sketches of structures. The trip to Istanbul in 1911 is emblematic, with the evocative representation of the landscape where the peaks of the Suleymaniye Camii, and the Fatih Mosque, are reflected in the shadow of the Golden Horn to the horizon marked by the line of the Sea of Marmara. The depth is hidden by the surface and, in order to get closer and understand, we have to describe rather than explain. The eyes are the mirror of the soul of the artist that allow, through the complete vision of the event, to enjoy the view of other worlds. The work is a witness of what we are looking for. The creative process takes a course that from visual diary, what we see with our eyes, is then processed by the mind and later reproduced by hand. The detail of the particular never loses sight of the overall vision. The education of Sergey Kuznetsov, born in Moscow, where he graduated in Architecture and where he mainly operates since 2006 in collaboration with Sergei Tchoban, highlights this ability, as readers can also see from the drawings published here, to use a modern language in accordance with tradition.
Massimiliano Fuksas

Luca Molinari

A Dialogue with Sergey Kuznetsov

LM: *As a designer, you have invested a significant amount of time making hundreds of drawings within the last two decades. What does drawing mean to you? When did you begin to consider drawing as a relevant part of your background and education?*
SK: Drawing has always been for me an inner, constant need, but a turning point in my understanding of the role of the drawing, perhaps, was while I prepared to enter college. It is important to note that at the Moscow Architectural Institute and the Russian School of Architecture, in general, traditionally a lot of attention is paid to working with your hands – and it's not just about drawing, but also sculptural work, painting, modelling, prototyping, drafting. National architectural education is still based on this. And although to many people it seems archaic, I personally think it is very useful. It is through the work of your hands that you better understand and feel proportion and space. And although my institute years are long gone, I'm still using drawing as a primary means of learning about architecture and with the assistance of drawing constantly discovering new aspects of it. Drawing was and remains for me perhaps the most convenient language that allows architectural impressions and thoughts to be communicated about this or that structure.

LM: *Analysing your drawings, I cannot find a direct relationship with your work, but I am sure that your research on drawings nurtures your research as a designer. Could you explain how drawing fosters and influences your design process?*
SK: Drawing helps to structure the impressions of architectural structures, because in the process of drawing, I analyse not only the compositional and decorative techniques, but also how to work with the materials, textures, etc. And this, in turn, helps to better understand the meaning of the structure, decoration, and how structural and decorative elements coexist and "work" together. Of course, this does not mean that later in my work I just copy some techniques. It's just that when you look and draw a lot, all of this quite to the contrary is stored in your head and then is reflected in your work. For instance, drawing gothic cathedrals with their repetitive arcades directly influenced the design of the Kazan Palace of Water Sports. This site is an absolute rhyme to the theme of a repeating arcade with rose windows and a coloured stained glass window at the end.

LM: *Studying your drawings, a relationship and a form of continuity with the generations of Russian artists and architects who considered Italy and Europe as a centre for their research and inspiration is evident. Do you feel this continuity? And which kind of relationship do you perceive with contemporary experiences?*
SK: Indeed, Russian artists and architects have always studied Italy. And the exhibition *Only Italy!* in the Tretyakov Gallery narrates exactly that. And in general, everything about Italy is clear: it is there that examples of ancient culture and architecture are located, those that have always been at the heart of academic education, not only in Russia but also in other countries. The roots of classical architecture in many countries, of course, are found in Italy, so it is not surprising that many generations of architects came there to study "primary sources". In terms of education, learning by primary experience is always more valuable than by derivatives, although derivatives are also very interesting. Personally, I find in Italy a source of inspiration and plentiful opportunities to explore outdoor scenes. Of course,

many outstanding graphics have been drawn not only of Italy: there are many very interesting drawings of works of Soviet or American architecture, or for instance, Mexican, too. In the world, in general, there are so many buildings of interest to graphic artists, but the Italian classics, I believe, are the basis of everything.

LM: *As the Chief Architect of Moscow City, you're dealing with redefining urban spaces and strategies for the city of the future. Which kind of relationship should there be between your research through drawings and a contemporary vision of urban space?*
SK: There is no point in making drawing a universal means of studying and designing everything. It's just that the city in which we draw is usually arranged very sensibly in terms of the organization of public spaces. The monuments there attract a huge number of people, and how the space around these structures is organized, how the streams of tourists and residents are distributed, and how historic and modern buildings interact with each other – all of this is memorized and analysed in the process of drawing and concurrently with it. In other words, by drawing, you travel and see a lot, these examples are collected and stored, and then they can easily be brought out in your work.

LM: *I feel that for you drawing is a personal, joyful obsession. Could you describe your approach over one day devoted to drawing? How and why do you choose the point of view and the positioning of your drawings?*
SK: Drawing is certainly a means of recreation and relaxation. The place is chosen by a very simple principle – it's desirable to find an unconventional view of even the most well-known buildings, plus it's interesting through the perspective and volume spatial arrangement of the drawing to reveal some intriguing features of the monument. They may be exaggerated in the drawing and different from reality. Drawing is not always the repetition of reality; it is a kind of delivery of an effect that produces a building (or group of buildings) for the viewer, in this case, for me. And some things I often do deliberately differently than they are in life, in order to emphasize the magnitude of the effect.

LM: *Which role should drawing play in the architectural education and in the architect's training today?*
SK: I'm certain that drawing is a key element of architectural education. Not to practice drawing which is taught to you is like learning a subject and not knowing the language. I believe that drawing is an absolutely essential skill with which one needs to start an education and needs to develop throughout a career. I think in today's architectural education by no means should the culture of working with your hands be neglected. Before a designer starts working with a computer, he must understand the laws by which a composition is constructed, by which light falls, and by which volume, shape and space are created. And for architects there is no better way to experience this than through drawing.

Venice, Italy, 2014
Charcoal pencil on paper, 56 × 42 cm

Drawings

Ravenna, Italy, 2014
Ink, brush on paper, 42 × 56 cm

San Gaetano, Florence, Italy, 2012
Brown ink, brush on paper, 50.8 × 35.9 cm

Temple of Antoninus and Faustina, Rome, Italy, 2008
Pencil on paper, 38.2 × 27.8 cm

Pantheon, Rome, Italy, 2008
Sanguine on paper, 29.8 × 41.7 cm

Arch of Constantine, Rome, Italy, 2009
Pencil, watercolour on paper, 40 × 59.7 cm

Santa Maria Formosa, Venice, Italy, 2011
Pencil on paper, 41 × 32 cm

Arch of Titus, Rome, Italy, 2007
Pencil on paper, 39 × 30.2 cm

Paris, France, 2011
Ink on paper, 41.8 × 29.6 cm

Madrid, Spain, 2011
Ink, sanguine on paper, 40 × 30 cm

Courtyard in Venice, Italy, 2014
Pencil on paper, 41.7 × 28.5 cm

Venice Biennale of Architecture,
Moscow: urban space, 2014
Pencil on paper, 41.8 × 28.5 cm

Santa Maria del Fiore, Florence, Italy, 2011
Pencil, pastel on grey paper, 38.8 × 29.2 cm

Piazza della Cisterna, San Gimignano, Italy, 2011
Pencil on paper, 31.2 × 23.2 cm

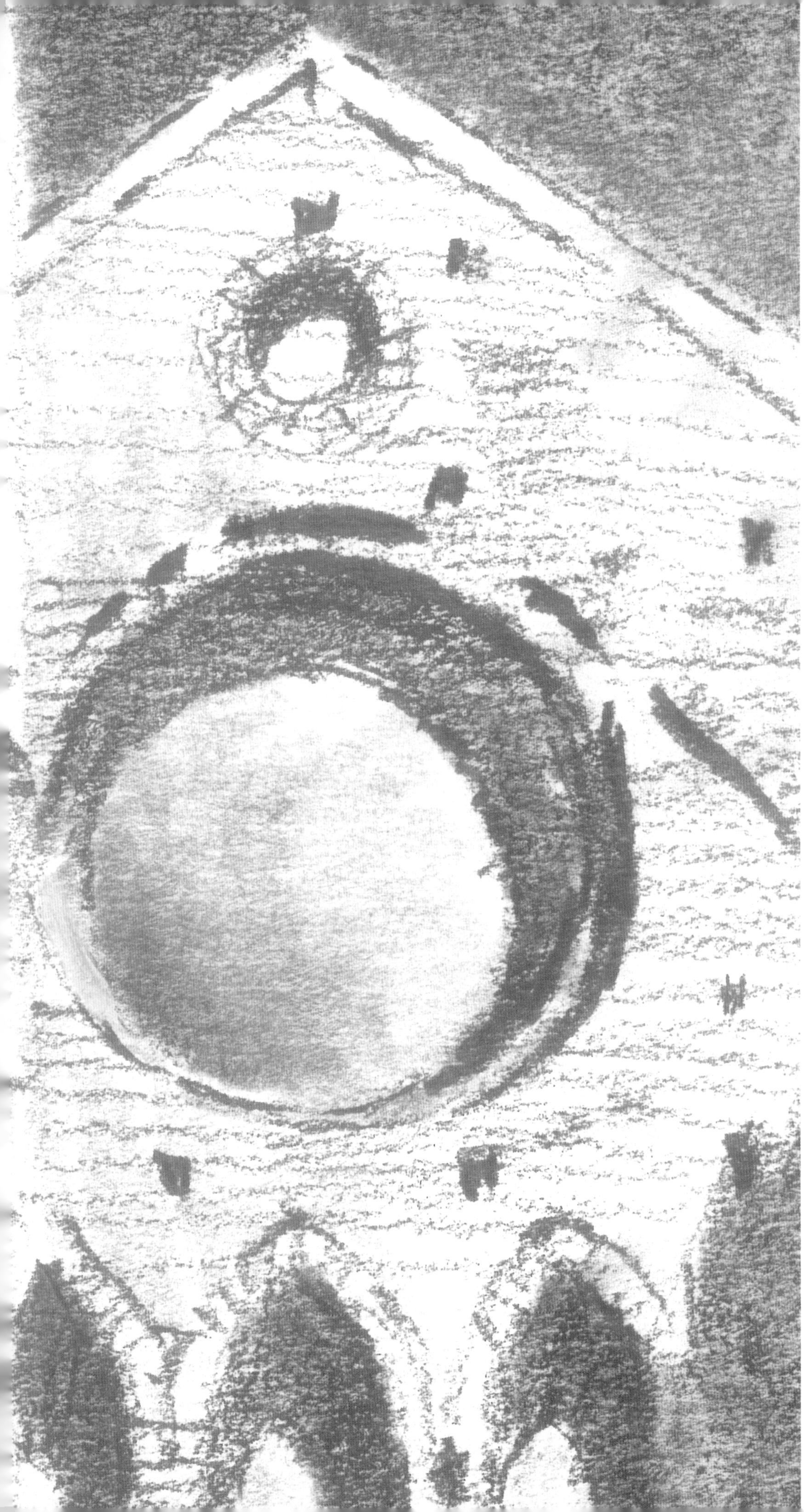

Abbey of San Galgano, Italy, 2011
Charcoal on paper, 40 × 30 cm

Siena, Italy, 2011
Pencil on paper, 30 × 40 cm

Piazza del Campo, Siena, Italy, 2011
Pencil on paper, 29.4 × 38.7 cm

Pisa Baptistery, Italy, 2012
Ink, brush on paper, 50.3 × 36 cm

Lucca Cathedral, Italy, 2014
Pencil, whiting on grey paper, 55 × 39.5 cm

Arena di Verona, Italy, 2011
Ink on paper, 30 × 42 cm

Santa Maria dei Miracoli, Venice, Italy, 2010
Pastel on paper, 41 × 28.5 cm

Basilica of Sant'Andrea, Mantua, Italy, 2014
Pencil on paper, 40 × 30.3 cm

HCL 8.03.2014

Verona, Italy, 2011
Ink, watercolour on paper, 41 × 53.2 cm

Bologna, Italy, 2014
Sepia, brush on paper, 38 × 54.6 cm

Vicenza, Italy, 2012
Pencil on paper, 30.2 × 40.5 cm

Campo Santa Maria Formosa, Venice, Italy, 2014
Brown ink on paper, 42 × 56 cm

Santa Maria della Salute, Venice, Italy, 2011
Pencil on paper, 32 × 40.4 cm

San Zaccaria, Venice, Italy, 2009
Ink on paper, 41 × 32 cm

Venice, Italy, 2011
Pencil, pastel on grey paper, 42 × 29.7 cm

Venice, Italy, 2010
Ink, watercolour on paper, 29.6 × 39.5 cm

San Antonio, Padua, Italy, 2010
Italian pencil on paper, 41.4 × 29.6 cm

San Fantin, Venice, Italy, 2010
Pencil on paper, 29.4 × 42 cm

Palazzo Malipiero, Venice, Italy, 2013
Ink, whiting on grey paper, 40 × 56.5 cm

Santa Maria della Salute, Venice, Italy, 2009
Pencil, pastel on grey paper, 32.2 × 25.2 cm

Santa Maria della Salute, Venice, Italy, 2010
Ink on paper, 42 × 30 cm

Architectural capriccio, Venice, 2008
Ink, watercolour on paper, 59.6 × 39.5 cm

Salt warehouses in Cervia, Italy, 2014
Pencil on paper, 28.6 × 42 cm

Campo Santa Maria Formosa, Venice, Italy, 2014
Charcoal pencil on paper, 42 × 56 cm

Venezia 07.2014.

San Giovanni e Paolo, Venice, Italy, 2010
Ink on paper, 30 × 42 cm

Nice, France, 2013
Ink, whiting on grey paper, 38 × 53.2 cm

Stockholm, 2011
Charcoal on paper, 29.2 × 21 cm

San Moise, Venice, Italy, 2008
Ink, watercolour on paper, 39.6 × 29.8 cm

The campo San Giovanni e Paolo, Venice, Italy, 2010
Ink, watercolour on paper, 29.7 × 41.5 cm

Bologna, Italy, 2014
Pencil on paper, 39.5 × 30.3 cm

Market in Rimini, Italy, 2014
Charcoal pencil on paper, 42 × 28.7 cm

Milan Cathedral, Italy, 2011
Ink on paper, 41 × 29 cm

Santa Maria presso San Satiro, Milan, Italy, 2011
Brown ink, brush on paper, 54.4 × 37 cm

Casa Mila, Barcelona, Spain, 2013
Brown ink, brush on paper, 29 × 39 cm

Barcelona, Spain, 2013
Brown ink, brush on paper, 28.8 × 38.5 cm

Cordoba, Spain, 2011
Coloured pencils on paper, 40 × 28.5 cm

Sagrada Familia, Barcelona, Spain, 2011
Ink on paper, 40 × 30 cm

Rouen Cathedral, France, 2011
Pastel on grey paper, 42 × 28.6 cm

Saint Louis Cathedral, Orléans, France, 2011
Pencil on paper, 40.1 × 31 cm

Rouen Cathedral, France, 2011
Ink on paper, 29.6 × 20.9 cm

Reims Cathedral, France, 2009
Pencil on paper, 39.2 × 28.8 cm

Rouen Cathedral, France, 2010
Ink on paper, 39.8 × 30 cm

Grand Place, Brussels, Belgium, 2013
Ink, brush, whiting on grey paper, 38.5 × 54.5 cm

Nice, France, 2013
Ink, brush, whiting on grey paper, 54.5 × 38.4 cm

Gamla Stan, Stockholm, Sweden, 2011
Ink on paper, 29.5 × 41.7 cm

Belfry of Bruges, Belgium, 2013
Brown ink, brush on paper, 54.5 × 38.3 cm

Budapest, Hungary, 2012
Pencil on paper, 41.8 × 29.2 cm

Krakow, Poland, 2012
Pencil on paper, 42 × 29 cm

Old Town Market Place, Warsaw, Poland, 2012
Pencil on paper, 28.8 × 41 cm

Mont Saint-Michel, France, 2011
Pencil, pastel on grey paper, 40.9 × 28.9 cm

Old embankment of Ghent, Belgium, 2013
Ink, brush, whiting on grey paper, 38.4 × 54.7 cm

Meribel, France, 2008
Pencil, watercolour on paper, 39.5 × 31.8 cm

Osthafen, Berlin, Germany, 2014
Pencil, whiting on grey paper, 39 × 55.3 cm

Paris, France, 2011
Pencil on paper, 39 × 29 cm

Mirsky Castle, Belorussia, 2012
Pencil on paper, 42 × 29.4 cm

Ukraina Hotel, Moscow, 2014
Sepia, brush on paper, 53 × 70 cm

Building in Moscow. Design sketch for the project, 2010
Pencil on paper, 41.2 × 29.5 cm

Factory in Vladivostok, Russia, 2010
Pencil on paper, 29.5 × 41.4 cm

Factory in Vladivostok, Russia, 2010
Pencil on paper, 29.5 × 41.1 cm

Vishny Volochek, Russia, 2010
Pencil on paper, 29.7 × 41 cm

Vishny Volochek, Russia, 2010
Pencil on paper, 41.6 × 29.5 cm

Vishny Volochek, Russia, 2010
Pencil on paper, 41.8 × 29.5 cm

The Ivan the Great Bell Tower, Moscow, 2013
Ink, brush, whiting on grey paper, 54.4 × 38.8 cm

Exhibition of Achievements of National Economy,
The pavilion of Meat Industry, Moscow, 2013
Ink, brush, whiting on grey paper, 54.5 × 38.3 cm

Exhibition of Achievements of National Economy, The Mechanization Pavilion, Moscow, 2013
Ink, brush, whiting on grey paper, 39 × 54 cm

Tchaikovsky Concert Hall, Moscow, 2014
Ink, brush, watercolour on paper, 54 × 74 cm

Сергей Кузнецов, 2014г.

Vishny Volochek, Russia, 2010
Pencil on paper, 29.6 × 41.3 cm

Tbilisi, Georgia, 2014
Pencil on paper, 21 × 29.7 cm

С.К. 03.08.2014
Тбилиси

Tokyo, Japan, 2013
Pencil on paper, 32 × 40.9 cm

Singapore, 2013
Felt-tip pen on paper, 30.5 × 40.5 cm

Singapore, 2013
Felt-tip pen on paper, 30.5 × 40.5 cm

Business center Moscow-City, Moscow, 2014
Felt-tip pens on paper, 42 × 57 cm

Kyoto, Japan, 2013
Pencil on paper, 29 × 39.5 cm

Kyoto, Japan, 2013
Pencil on paper, 39 × 28.7 cm

Miami, Florida, USA, 2014
Felt-tip pen on paper, 29 × 41.7 cm

CONGRESS
HOTEL
7.01.2014
С.К. Майами, Флорида

Arkadi Monastery, Crete, Greece, 2011
Pencil on paper, 21 × 30 cm

Mexico City, Mexico, 2012
Brown ink, brush on paper, 53 × 37.3 cm

Pyramid at Teotihuacan, Mexico, 2012
Brown ink, brush on paper, 36.5 × 53 cm

Houston, Texas, USA, 2014
Ink, brush on paper, 38.5 × 54.6 cm

С.К. Хьюстон, Техас
11.01.2014

Miami, Florida, USA, 2014
Ink, brush on paper, 38.5 × 54.5 cm

42nd Street, New York City, USA, 2012
Pencil on paper, 29.5 × 41.9 cm

High Line, New York City, USA, 2011
Pencil on paper, 20.4 × 29 cm

Chicago, USA, 2011
Pencil, ink on paper, 39 × 29 cm

Wall Street and Trinity Church, New York City, USA, 2009
Pencil on paper, 29.4 × 20.8 cm

5th Avenue / Park Street, New York City, USA, 200[illegible]
Pencil on paper, 29.2 × 20.8 cm

New York City, USA, 2009
Pencil, ink on paper, 20.3 × 30 cm

Architectural capriccio "New York City", 2011–2012
Pencil on paper, 29.5 × 42 cm

New York City, USA, 2009
Ink on paper, 39.8 × 29 cm

New York City, USA, 2014
Felt-tip pen on paper, 38.5 × 54.5 cm

THE

New York City, USA, 2014
Felt-tip pens on paper, 38.5 × 54.5 cm

CNN

New York City, USA, 2014
Ink, brush on paper, 55 × 38.5 cm

Е.К. Н.Й. 07.01.2014

Houston, Texas, USA, 2014
Ink, brush on paper, 38.7 × 55 cm

Plaza Hotel in New York City, USA, 2013
Pencil on paper, 29 × 41.5 cm

New York City, USA, 2014
Coloured pencils on paper, 42 × 56 cm

New York City, USA, 2014
Charcoal pencil, coloured pencils on paper,
42 × 56 cm

New York City, USA, 2014
Charcoal pencil, coloured pencils on paper,
42 × 56 cm

New York City, USA, 2014
Charcoal pencil on paper, 42 × 56 cm

NY 2014.10

Clouds, Vishny Volochek, Russia, 2010
Pencil on paper, 29.5 × 41.6 cm

Clouds, Vishny Volochek, Russia, 2010
Pencil on paper, 29.6 × 41.3 cm

Hagia Sophia, Istanbul, Turkey, 2014
Pencil, whiting on paper, 42 × 59.7 cm

Architectural capriccio, 2010
Pencil on paper, 41.5 × 29.5 cm

Design sketch for the embankment in Kazan, Tatarstan, Russian Federation, 2011–2012
Coloured pencils on paper, 29.5 × 42 cm

Design sketch for the embankment in Kazan, Tatarstan, Russian Federation, 2011–2012
Coloured pencils on paper, 29.5 × 42 cm

Design sketch for the embankment in Kazan, Tatarstan, Russian Federation, 2011–2012
Coloured pencils on paper, 29.5 × 42 cm

Design sketch for the embankment in Kazan, Tatarstan, Russian Federation, 2011–2012
Coloured pencils on paper, 29.5 × 42 cm

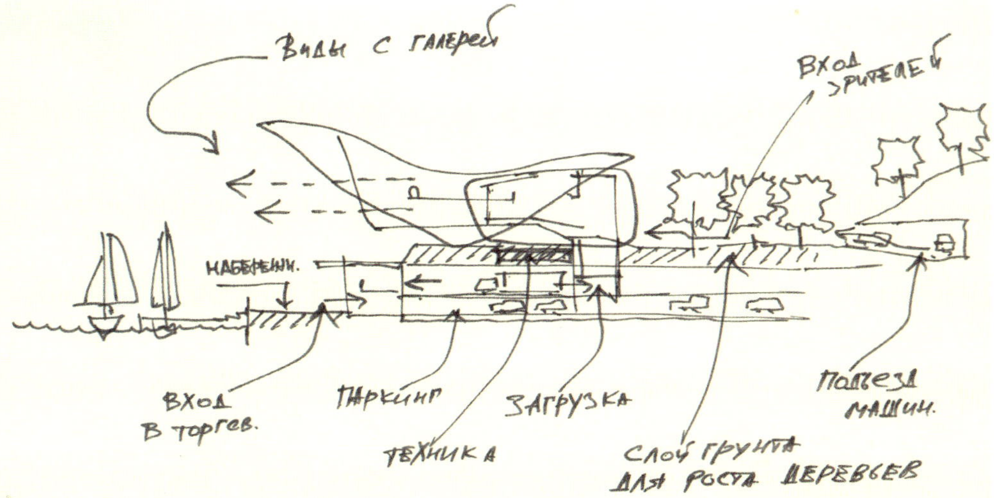
Виды с галерей
Вход зрителей
Набережн.
Вход в торгов.
Паркинг
Загрузка
Подъезд машин.
Техника
Слой грунта для роста деревьев

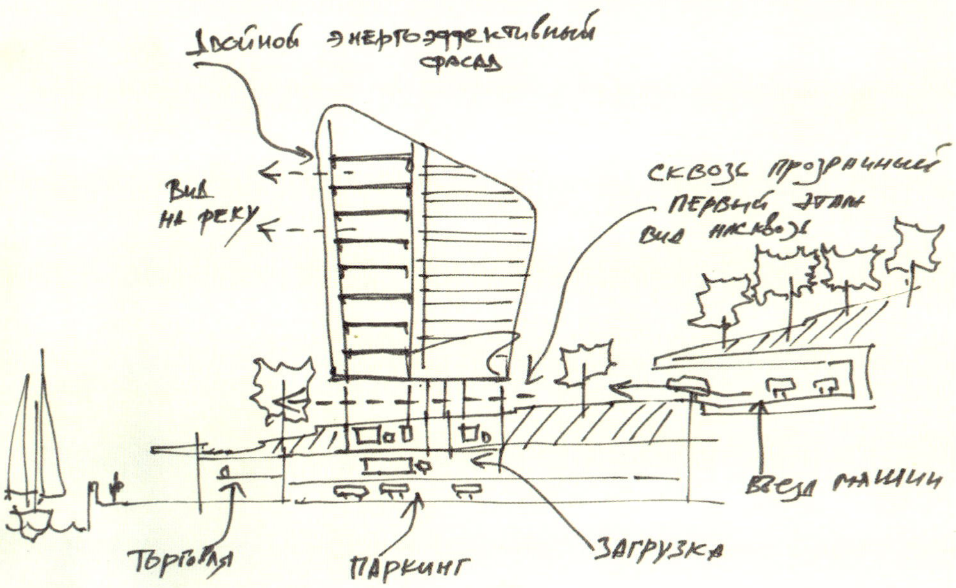
Двойной энергоэффективный фасад
Вид на реку
Сквозь прозрачный первый этаж вид насквозь
Въезд машин
Торговля
Паркинг
Загрузка

Biography

Sergey Kuznetsov was born in 1977 in Moscow. In 2001 he graduated from the Moscow Architectural Institute. In the final course of study, he already founded his first architectural studio that was in close collaboration with a German studio nps tchoban voss, headed by Russian-German architect Sergei Tchoban. In 2006 Sergey Kuznetsov and Sergei Tchoban founded the office SPEECH Tchoban & Kuznetsov. It quickly became successful in Russia and currently has 250 employees. SPEECH Tchoban & Kuznetsov has authored such projects as Office Building on Leninsky prospekt (Moscow), Residential complex Granatny 6 (Moscow), Grunewald Residential complex (Moscow), Office and Business multifunctional complex on Ozerkovskaya embankment (Moscow), Palace of Water Sports (Kazan), Museum for Architectural Drawing in Berlin, Hotel Kempinski Plaza in Minsk, Republic of Belarus.
Kuznetsov has taken part in various architecture exhibitions, including international ones. In 2010 and 2012 he was the co-curator of the Russian pavilion at the Venice Architecture Biennale, which for the first time was awarded with an "Honourable Mention" prize by the jury in 2012. Since 2008 Kuznetsov is also an editor for *speech: architectural magazine*. In 2012 Kuznetsov was assigned to the post of the Chief Architect of Moscow and he left his partnership at SPEECH. Today Kuznetsov is eager to actively increase the quality of architecture in Moscow. He applies a competitive practice with foreign experts, changes the quality of standard social objects and public spaces and indulges in educational and publishing projects.

Completed Projects

2013
Museum for Architectural Drawing, Tchoban Foundation, new exhibition building, Berlin
Palace of Water Sports, new aquatic stadium for the World University Games 2013, Kazan

2012
Russian pavilion at the XIII Architecture Biennale in Venice
Installation *Architect's eye* at *Interni Legacy* exhibition in Milan

2011
Bank St Petersburg Plaza, urban master plan and new administrative headquarters, in collaboration with Evgeny Gerasimov EGP St Petersburg, St Petersburg
Business multifunctional complex Aquamarine on Ozerkovskaya embankment new business complex, Moscow
VTB, office interior in the Western tower of the Federation Complex, Moscow

2010
Five Seas, A-class business centre, Rostov
Office building on Leninsky prospekt, Moscow
Residential complex Granatny 6, new residential complex, Moscow
Residential complex Grunewald, Skolkovskoye Shosse, new residential complex, Moscow

2008
Megatorg, new shopping centre, Vladimir

Current Projects

East Tower of the Federation Complex, Moscow (completion 2014)
Expo-Gate, new trade fair centre, St Petersburg (completion 2014)
Nevskaya Ratusha, new administration complex for the city of St Petersburg (completion 2014)

Awards

2014
Honourable Mention, AIT Award 2014 (Germany) for the Museum for Architectural Drawing in Berlin

2013
Best of Best of the Iconic Awards 2013 by the German Design Council, Frankfurt, for building of the Museum for Architectural Drawing in Berlin
Ar+d Awards for Emerging Architecture 2013, United Kingdom
Architectural Review future Projects Awards 2013 for the project Museum for Architectural Drawing in Berlin

2012
Honourable Mention, Award at the XIII Architecture Biennale 2012 in Venice for the exhibition *i-city / i-land*
Five Stars Best Office Architecture at International Property Awards 2012 for the office building on Leninsky prospekt, Moscow
Honourable Mention Award in the Architecture Multiple Residence category at the International Property Awards 2012 for the residential complex Granatny 6, Moscow
Commercial Real Estate St Petersburg Award 2012, Best Business Centre, Class A for the Bank St Petersburg Plaza complex in collaboration with Evgeny Gerasimov and partners, St Petersburg
Architect of the Year (title), at the III Architecture Biennale in Moscow and XVII Exhibition for Architecture and Design *Arch Moskva* in collaboration with Sergei Tchoban and SPEECH Tchoban & Kuznetsov, Moscow
Grand Prix and Best Office Award 2012, Best Office for the Director for the interior design of the office space for VTB Bank in the Western tower of the Federation Complex, Moscow

2011
House of the Year 2011, Russia wide readers award for the office building at Leninsky prospekt, Moscow
Golden Diploma, First National Glass in Architecture award for the St Petersburg Plaza complex in collaboration with Evgeny Gerasimov and partners, St Petersburg

Exhibitions

2014
Only Italy! Architectural graphic art of the XVIII-XXIst centuries, State Tretyakov Gallery, Moscow; catalogue published

2013
Architectural drawing, exhibition for Architecture and Design *Arch Moskva 2013* in collaboration with Sergei Tchoban and SPEECH Tchoban & Kuznetsov, Moscow
New Moscow, Exhibition for Architecture and Design *Arch Moskva 2013*, Moscow

2012
MIPIM 2012, participation in the Moscow stand, Cannes
Moscow Design Week, participation with installation *Architect's eye* at the exhibition *Interni Legacy*, Milan
i-city/i-land, Russian pavilion at the XIII Venice Architecture Biennale, awarded with an Honourable Mention Mention, Venice; catalogue published
Milan Design Week, participation with installation *Architect's eye* at the exhibition *Interni Legacy*, Milan

2011
XIX International Zodchestvo Festival 2011, participation, Moscow
MIPIM 2011, participation in the Moscow stand, Cannes

2010
Factory Russia, co-curation, design, organization and participation in the exhibition of the Russian Pavilion at the XII Venice Architecture Biennale 2011, Venice; catalogue published
II Moscow Architecture Biennale, participation, Moscow

2009
New life of Sretenka. Renovation of historical quartier, AEDES Gallery, Berlin
Emergency Reserve. Industrial Architecture of the Past – a Resource for the Future, participation as part of the XVII International Zodchestvo Festival 2009, Manege exhibition hall, Moscow

2008
BERLIN MOSCOW, Fine Arts Museum, Sochi

2007
XII Arch Moskva Exhibition for Architecture and Design, participation, Central House of the Artist, Moscow

Publishing Activities

Only Italy! Architectural graphic art of the XVIII-XXIst centuries, Iskusstvo-XXI vek, Moscow, 2014
Tatlin_Mono. SPEECH Tchoban & Kuznetsov 2006-2013, monograph, Tatlin Publishers, 2013
SPEECH Tchoban & Kuznetsov, monograph, 2013